# TABLE OF CONTENTS

MW00933346

EVENT:

LOCATION:

**MAILING LIST**

DATE:   TIME:

| NAME | EMAIL | PHONE | NOTE |
|------|-------|-------|------|
| | | | |

MONTH:

| EVENT: | | | MAILING LIST |
|--------|--|--|--------------|

| LOCATION: | | DATE: | TIME: |
|-----------|--|-------|-------|

| NAME | EMAIL | PHONE | NOTE |
|------|-------|-------|------|
|  |  |  |  |
|  |  |  |  |
|  |  |  |  |
|  |  |  |  |
|  |  |  |  |
|  |  |  |  |
|  |  |  |  |
|  |  |  |  |
|  |  |  |  |
|  |  |  |  |
|  |  |  |  |
|  |  |  |  |
|  |  |  |  |
|  |  |  |  |
|  |  |  |  |
|  |  |  |  |
|  |  |  |  |
|  |  |  |  |
|  |  |  |  |
|  |  |  |  |
|  |  |  |  |
|  |  |  |  |
|  |  |  |  |
|  |  |  |  |
|  |  |  |  |

| EVENT: | | | MAILING LIST |
| LOCATION: | | | DATE: TIME: |

| NAME | EMAIL | PHONE | NOTE |
|------|-------|-------|------|
| | | | |
| | | | |
| | | | |
| | | | |
| | | | |
| | | | |
| | | | |
| | | | |
| | | | |
| | | | |
| | | | |
| | | | |
| | | | |
| | | | |
| | | | |
| | | | |
| | | | |
| | | | |
| | | | |
| | | | |
| | | | |
| | | | |

3

| EVENT: | | | MAILING LIST |
| LOCATION: | | | DATE:     TIME: |

| NAME | EMAIL | PHONE | NOTE |
|------|-------|-------|------|
|  |  |  |  |
|  |  |  |  |
|  |  |  |  |
|  |  |  |  |
|  |  |  |  |
|  |  |  |  |
|  |  |  |  |
|  |  |  |  |
|  |  |  |  |
|  |  |  |  |
|  |  |  |  |
|  |  |  |  |
|  |  |  |  |
|  |  |  |  |
|  |  |  |  |
|  |  |  |  |
|  |  |  |  |
|  |  |  |  |
|  |  |  |  |
|  |  |  |  |
|  |  |  |  |
|  |  |  |  |
|  |  |  |  |

| EVENT: | | | MAILING LIST |
| --- | --- | --- | --- |
| LOCATION: | | | DATE:     TIME: |

| NAME | EMAIL | PHONE | NOTE |
| --- | --- | --- | --- |
|  |  |  |  |
|  |  |  |  |
|  |  |  |  |
|  |  |  |  |
|  |  |  |  |
|  |  |  |  |
|  |  |  |  |
|  |  |  |  |
|  |  |  |  |
|  |  |  |  |
|  |  |  |  |
|  |  |  |  |
|  |  |  |  |
|  |  |  |  |
|  |  |  |  |
|  |  |  |  |
|  |  |  |  |
|  |  |  |  |
|  |  |  |  |
|  |  |  |  |
|  |  |  |  |
|  |  |  |  |
|  |  |  |  |

| EVENT: | | | MAILING LIST |
| --- | --- | --- | --- |
| LOCATION: | | | DATE: TIME: |

| NAME | EMAIL | PHONE | NOTE |
| --- | --- | --- | --- |
| | | | |
| | | | |
| | | | |
| | | | |
| | | | |
| | | | |
| | | | |
| | | | |
| | | | |
| | | | |
| | | | |
| | | | |
| | | | |
| | | | |
| | | | |
| | | | |
| | | | |
| | | | |
| | | | |
| | | | |
| | | | |
| | | | |
| | | | |
| | | | |

| EVENT: | | MAILING LIST | |
|---|---|---|---|
| LOCATION: | | DATE: | TIME: |

| NAME | EMAIL | PHONE | NOTE |
|---|---|---|---|
| | | | |
| | | | |
| | | | |
| | | | |
| | | | |
| | | | |
| | | | |
| | | | |
| | | | |
| | | | |
| | | | |
| | | | |
| | | | |
| | | | |
| | | | |
| | | | |
| | | | |
| | | | |
| | | | |
| | | | |
| | | | |
| | | | |
| | | | |
| | | | |
| | | | |
| | | | |

| EVENT: | | | MAILING LIST |
| --- | --- | --- | --- |
| LOCATION: | | DATE: | TIME: |

| NAME | EMAIL | PHONE | NOTE |
| --- | --- | --- | --- |
| | | | |
| | | | |
| | | | |
| | | | |
| | | | |
| | | | |
| | | | |
| | | | |
| | | | |
| | | | |
| | | | |
| | | | |
| | | | |
| | | | |
| | | | |
| | | | |
| | | | |
| | | | |
| | | | |
| | | | |
| | | | |
| | | | |
| | | | |
| | | | |
| | | | |

| EVENT: | | | MAILING LIST |
| LOCATION: | | | DATE: TIME: |

| NAME | EMAIL | PHONE | NOTE |
| --- | --- | --- | --- |
| | | | |
| | | | |
| | | | |
| | | | |
| | | | |
| | | | |
| | | | |
| | | | |
| | | | |
| | | | |
| | | | |
| | | | |
| | | | |
| | | | |
| | | | |
| | | | |
| | | | |
| | | | |
| | | | |
| | | | |
| | | | |
| | | | |
| | | | |
| | | | |

| EVENT: | | | |
|---|---|---|---|
| **LOCATION:** | | DATE: | TIME: |

**MAILING LIST**

| NAME | EMAIL | PHONE | NOTE |
|---|---|---|---|
| | | | |
| | | | |
| | | | |
| | | | |
| | | | |
| | | | |
| | | | |
| | | | |
| | | | |
| | | | |
| | | | |
| | | | |
| | | | |
| | | | |
| | | | |
| | | | |
| | | | |
| | | | |
| | | | |
| | | | |
| | | | |
| | | | |
| | | | |
| | | | |
| | | | |
| | | | |
| | | | |

| EVENT: | | MAILING LIST | |
|--------|--|--------------|--|
| **LOCATION:** | | **DATE:** **TIME:** | |

| NAME | EMAIL | PHONE | NOTE |
|------|-------|-------|------|
|  |  |  |  |
|  |  |  |  |
|  |  |  |  |
|  |  |  |  |
|  |  |  |  |
|  |  |  |  |
|  |  |  |  |
|  |  |  |  |
|  |  |  |  |
|  |  |  |  |
|  |  |  |  |
|  |  |  |  |
|  |  |  |  |
|  |  |  |  |
|  |  |  |  |
|  |  |  |  |
|  |  |  |  |
|  |  |  |  |
|  |  |  |  |
|  |  |  |  |
|  |  |  |  |
|  |  |  |  |

| EVENT: | | | | MAILING LIST |
|---|---|---|---|---|

| LOCATION: | | | DATE:  TIME: |
|---|---|---|---|

| NAME | EMAIL | PHONE | NOTE |
|---|---|---|---|
| | | | |
| | | | |
| | | | |
| | | | |
| | | | |
| | | | |
| | | | |
| | | | |
| | | | |
| | | | |
| | | | |
| | | | |
| | | | |
| | | | |
| | | | |
| | | | |
| | | | |
| | | | |
| | | | |
| | | | |
| | | | |
| | | | |
| | | | |
| | | | |

| EVENT: | | | |
|---|---|---|---|

**MAILING LIST**

| LOCATION: | | DATE: | TIME: |
|---|---|---|---|

| NAME | EMAIL | PHONE | NOTE |
|---|---|---|---|
| | | | |
| | | | |
| | | | |
| | | | |
| | | | |
| | | | |
| | | | |
| | | | |
| | | | |
| | | | |
| | | | |
| | | | |
| | | | |
| | | | |
| | | | |
| | | | |
| | | | |
| | | | |
| | | | |
| | | | |
| | | | |
| | | | |
| | | | |

| EVENT: | | | MAILING LIST |
|--------|--|--|--------------|
| **LOCATION:** | | | **DATE:    TIME:** |

| NAME | EMAIL | PHONE | NOTE |
|------|-------|-------|------|
|  |  |  |  |
|  |  |  |  |
|  |  |  |  |
|  |  |  |  |
|  |  |  |  |
|  |  |  |  |
|  |  |  |  |
|  |  |  |  |
|  |  |  |  |
|  |  |  |  |
|  |  |  |  |
|  |  |  |  |
|  |  |  |  |
|  |  |  |  |
|  |  |  |  |
|  |  |  |  |
|  |  |  |  |
|  |  |  |  |
|  |  |  |  |
|  |  |  |  |
|  |  |  |  |
|  |  |  |  |
|  |  |  |  |

| EVENT: | | | MAILING LIST |
| --- | --- | --- | --- |
| LOCATION: | | | DATE:    TIME: |

| NAME | EMAIL | PHONE | NOTE |
| --- | --- | --- | --- |
| | | | |
| | | | |
| | | | |
| | | | |
| | | | |
| | | | |
| | | | |
| | | | |
| | | | |
| | | | |
| | | | |
| | | | |
| | | | |
| | | | |
| | | | |
| | | | |
| | | | |
| | | | |
| | | | |
| | | | |
| | | | |
| | | | |
| | | | |

| EVENT: | | MAILING LIST | |
|---|---|---|---|
| LOCATION: | | DATE: | TIME: |

| NAME | EMAIL | PHONE | NOTE |
|---|---|---|---|
| | | | |
| | | | |
| | | | |
| | | | |
| | | | |
| | | | |
| | | | |
| | | | |
| | | | |
| | | | |
| | | | |
| | | | |
| | | | |
| | | | |
| | | | |
| | | | |
| | | | |
| | | | |
| | | | |
| | | | |
| | | | |
| | | | |
| | | | |

**EVENT:**

**LOCATION:**

**DATE:** **TIME:**

| NAME | EMAIL | PHONE | NOTE |
|------|-------|-------|------|
|      |       |       |      |
|      |       |       |      |
|      |       |       |      |
|      |       |       |      |
|      |       |       |      |
|      |       |       |      |
|      |       |       |      |
|      |       |       |      |
|      |       |       |      |
|      |       |       |      |
|      |       |       |      |
|      |       |       |      |
|      |       |       |      |
|      |       |       |      |
|      |       |       |      |
|      |       |       |      |
|      |       |       |      |
|      |       |       |      |
|      |       |       |      |
|      |       |       |      |
|      |       |       |      |

**EVENT:**

**LOCATION:**

**DATE:**     **TIME:**

| NAME | EMAIL | PHONE | NOTE |
|------|-------|-------|------|
|      |       |       |      |
|      |       |       |      |
|      |       |       |      |
|      |       |       |      |
|      |       |       |      |
|      |       |       |      |
|      |       |       |      |
|      |       |       |      |
|      |       |       |      |
|      |       |       |      |
|      |       |       |      |
|      |       |       |      |
|      |       |       |      |
|      |       |       |      |
|      |       |       |      |
|      |       |       |      |
|      |       |       |      |
|      |       |       |      |
|      |       |       |      |
|      |       |       |      |
|      |       |       |      |
|      |       |       |      |
|      |       |       |      |
|      |       |       |      |
|      |       |       |      |

| EVENT: | | MAILING LIST | |
|---|---|---|---|
| LOCATION: | | DATE: TIME: | |

| NAME | EMAIL | PHONE | NOTE |
|---|---|---|---|
| | | | |
| | | | |
| | | | |
| | | | |
| | | | |
| | | | |
| | | | |
| | | | |
| | | | |
| | | | |
| | | | |
| | | | |
| | | | |
| | | | |
| | | | |
| | | | |
| | | | |
| | | | |
| | | | |
| | | | |
| | | | |
| | | | |

**EVENT:**

**LOCATION:**

## MAILING LIST

**DATE:**    **TIME:**

| NAME | EMAIL | PHONE | NOTE |
|------|-------|-------|------|
|  |  |  |  |
|  |  |  |  |
|  |  |  |  |
|  |  |  |  |
|  |  |  |  |
|  |  |  |  |
|  |  |  |  |
|  |  |  |  |
|  |  |  |  |
|  |  |  |  |
|  |  |  |  |
|  |  |  |  |
|  |  |  |  |
|  |  |  |  |
|  |  |  |  |
|  |  |  |  |
|  |  |  |  |
|  |  |  |  |
|  |  |  |  |
|  |  |  |  |
|  |  |  |  |
|  |  |  |  |
|  |  |  |  |
|  |  |  |  |
|  |  |  |  |

| EVENT: | | | MAILING LIST |
| --- | --- | --- | --- |
| LOCATION: | | | DATE:  TIME: |

| NAME | EMAIL | PHONE | NOTE |
| --- | --- | --- | --- |
| | | | |
| | | | |
| | | | |
| | | | |
| | | | |
| | | | |
| | | | |
| | | | |
| | | | |
| | | | |
| | | | |
| | | | |
| | | | |
| | | | |
| | | | |
| | | | |
| | | | |
| | | | |
| | | | |
| | | | |
| | | | |
| | | | |
| | | | |
| | | | |
| | | | |
| | | | |

| EVENT: | | | MAILING LIST |
| --- | --- | --- | --- |
| LOCATION: | | | DATE:     TIME: |

| NAME | EMAIL | PHONE | NOTE |
| --- | --- | --- | --- |
|  |  |  |  |
|  |  |  |  |
|  |  |  |  |
|  |  |  |  |
|  |  |  |  |
|  |  |  |  |
|  |  |  |  |
|  |  |  |  |
|  |  |  |  |
|  |  |  |  |
|  |  |  |  |
|  |  |  |  |
|  |  |  |  |
|  |  |  |  |
|  |  |  |  |
|  |  |  |  |
|  |  |  |  |
|  |  |  |  |
|  |  |  |  |
|  |  |  |  |
|  |  |  |  |
|  |  |  |  |
|  |  |  |  |
|  |  |  |  |
|  |  |  |  |

| EVENT: | | | MAILING LIST |
|--------|--|--|--------------|

| LOCATION: | | DATE: | TIME: |
|-----------|--|-------|-------|

| NAME | EMAIL | PHONE | NOTE |
|------|-------|-------|------|
|  |  |  |  |
|  |  |  |  |
|  |  |  |  |
|  |  |  |  |
|  |  |  |  |
|  |  |  |  |
|  |  |  |  |
|  |  |  |  |
|  |  |  |  |
|  |  |  |  |
|  |  |  |  |
|  |  |  |  |
|  |  |  |  |
|  |  |  |  |
|  |  |  |  |
|  |  |  |  |
|  |  |  |  |
|  |  |  |  |
|  |  |  |  |
|  |  |  |  |
|  |  |  |  |
|  |  |  |  |
|  |  |  |  |
|  |  |  |  |

**EVENT:**

**LOCATION:**

**MAILING LIST**

**DATE:**     **TIME:**

| NAME | EMAIL | PHONE | NOTE |
|------|-------|-------|------|
|      |       |       |      |
|      |       |       |      |
|      |       |       |      |
|      |       |       |      |
|      |       |       |      |
|      |       |       |      |
|      |       |       |      |
|      |       |       |      |
|      |       |       |      |
|      |       |       |      |
|      |       |       |      |
|      |       |       |      |
|      |       |       |      |
|      |       |       |      |
|      |       |       |      |
|      |       |       |      |
|      |       |       |      |
|      |       |       |      |
|      |       |       |      |
|      |       |       |      |
|      |       |       |      |
|      |       |       |      |
|      |       |       |      |

| EVENT: | | **MAILING LIST** | |
|--------|--|------------------|--|
| LOCATION: | | DATE:      TIME: | |

| NAME | EMAIL | PHONE | NOTE |
|------|-------|-------|------|
| | | | |
| | | | |
| | | | |
| | | | |
| | | | |
| | | | |
| | | | |
| | | | |
| | | | |
| | | | |
| | | | |
| | | | |
| | | | |
| | | | |
| | | | |
| | | | |
| | | | |
| | | | |
| | | | |
| | | | |
| | | | |
| | | | |
| | | | |
| | | | |
| | | | |
| | | | |
| | | | |

**EVENT:**

**LOCATION:**

**DATE:**   **TIME:**

| NAME | EMAIL | PHONE | NOTE |
|------|-------|-------|------|
|      |       |       |      |
|      |       |       |      |
|      |       |       |      |
|      |       |       |      |
|      |       |       |      |
|      |       |       |      |
|      |       |       |      |
|      |       |       |      |
|      |       |       |      |
|      |       |       |      |
|      |       |       |      |
|      |       |       |      |
|      |       |       |      |
|      |       |       |      |
|      |       |       |      |
|      |       |       |      |
|      |       |       |      |
|      |       |       |      |
|      |       |       |      |
|      |       |       |      |
|      |       |       |      |
|      |       |       |      |
|      |       |       |      |
|      |       |       |      |

| EVENT: | | | | MAILING LIST |
|--------|--|--|--|--------------|

| LOCATION: | | DATE: TIME: |
|-----------|--|-------------|

| NAME | EMAIL | PHONE | NOTE |
|------|-------|-------|------|
|  |  |  |  |
|  |  |  |  |
|  |  |  |  |
|  |  |  |  |
|  |  |  |  |
|  |  |  |  |
|  |  |  |  |
|  |  |  |  |
|  |  |  |  |
|  |  |  |  |
|  |  |  |  |
|  |  |  |  |
|  |  |  |  |
|  |  |  |  |
|  |  |  |  |
|  |  |  |  |
|  |  |  |  |
|  |  |  |  |
|  |  |  |  |
|  |  |  |  |
|  |  |  |  |
|  |  |  |  |
|  |  |  |  |
|  |  |  |  |

| EVENT: | | | MAILING LIST |
| --- | --- | --- | --- |
| LOCATION: | | | DATE:    TIME: |

| NAME | EMAIL | PHONE | NOTE |
| --- | --- | --- | --- |
| | | | |
| | | | |
| | | | |
| | | | |
| | | | |
| | | | |
| | | | |
| | | | |
| | | | |
| | | | |
| | | | |
| | | | |
| | | | |
| | | | |
| | | | |
| | | | |
| | | | |
| | | | |
| | | | |
| | | | |
| | | | |
| | | | |
| | | | |
| | | | |

**EVENT:**

**LOCATION:**

**MAILING LIST**

**DATE:**     **TIME:**

| NAME | EMAIL | PHONE | NOTE |
|---|---|---|---|
| | | | |
| | | | |
| | | | |
| | | | |
| | | | |
| | | | |
| | | | |
| | | | |
| | | | |
| | | | |
| | | | |
| | | | |
| | | | |
| | | | |
| | | | |
| | | | |
| | | | |
| | | | |
| | | | |
| | | | |
| | | | |
| | | | |
| | | | |
| | | | |
| | | | |
| | | | |

| EVENT: | | MAILING LIST | |
|---|---|---|---|
| LOCATION: | | DATE: TIME: | |

| NAME | EMAIL | PHONE | NOTE |
|---|---|---|---|
| | | | |
| | | | |
| | | | |
| | | | |
| | | | |
| | | | |
| | | | |
| | | | |
| | | | |
| | | | |
| | | | |
| | | | |
| | | | |
| | | | |
| | | | |
| | | | |
| | | | |
| | | | |
| | | | |
| | | | |
| | | | |
| | | | |
| | | | |

| EVENT: | | MAILING LIST | |
|---|---|---|---|
| LOCATION: | | DATE: | TIME: |

| NAME | EMAIL | PHONE | NOTE |
|---|---|---|---|
| | | | |
| | | | |
| | | | |
| | | | |
| | | | |
| | | | |
| | | | |
| | | | |
| | | | |
| | | | |
| | | | |
| | | | |
| | | | |
| | | | |
| | | | |
| | | | |
| | | | |
| | | | |
| | | | |
| | | | |
| | | | |
| | | | |
| | | | |

| EVENT: | | MAILING LIST | |
|--------|--|-------------|--|
| LOCATION: | | DATE: TIME: | |

| NAME | EMAIL | PHONE | NOTE |
|------|-------|-------|------|
| | | | |
| | | | |
| | | | |
| | | | |
| | | | |
| | | | |
| | | | |
| | | | |
| | | | |
| | | | |
| | | | |
| | | | |
| | | | |
| | | | |
| | | | |
| | | | |
| | | | |
| | | | |
| | | | |
| | | | |
| | | | |
| | | | |
| | | | |

| EVENT: | | **MAILING LIST** | |
|---|---|---|---|
| LOCATION: | | DATE: TIME: | |

| NAME | EMAIL | PHONE | NOTE |
|---|---|---|---|
| | | | |
| | | | |
| | | | |
| | | | |
| | | | |
| | | | |
| | | | |
| | | | |
| | | | |
| | | | |
| | | | |
| | | | |
| | | | |
| | | | |
| | | | |
| | | | |
| | | | |
| | | | |
| | | | |
| | | | |
| | | | |
| | | | |
| | | | |
| | | | |
| | | | |
| | | | |
| | | | |

| EVENT: | | MAILING LIST | |
|---|---|---|---|
| LOCATION: | | DATE: | TIME: |

| NAME | EMAIL | PHONE | NOTE |
|---|---|---|---|
|  |  |  |  |
|  |  |  |  |
|  |  |  |  |
|  |  |  |  |
|  |  |  |  |
|  |  |  |  |
|  |  |  |  |
|  |  |  |  |
|  |  |  |  |
|  |  |  |  |
|  |  |  |  |
|  |  |  |  |
|  |  |  |  |
|  |  |  |  |
|  |  |  |  |
|  |  |  |  |
|  |  |  |  |
|  |  |  |  |
|  |  |  |  |
|  |  |  |  |
|  |  |  |  |
|  |  |  |  |
|  |  |  |  |
|  |  |  |  |

| EVENT: | | | MAILING LIST |
|--------|--|--|--------------|

| LOCATION: | | DATE: | TIME: |
|-----------|--|-------|-------|

| NAME | EMAIL | PHONE | NOTE |
|------|-------|-------|------|
| | | | |
| | | | |
| | | | |
| | | | |
| | | | |
| | | | |
| | | | |
| | | | |
| | | | |
| | | | |
| | | | |
| | | | |
| | | | |
| | | | |
| | | | |
| | | | |
| | | | |
| | | | |
| | | | |
| | | | |
| | | | |
| | | | |
| | | | |
| | | | |

| EVENT: | | | MAILING LIST |
| --- | --- | --- | --- |
| LOCATION: | | DATE: | TIME: |

| NAME | EMAIL | PHONE | NOTE |
| --- | --- | --- | --- |
| | | | |
| | | | |
| | | | |
| | | | |
| | | | |
| | | | |
| | | | |
| | | | |
| | | | |
| | | | |
| | | | |
| | | | |
| | | | |
| | | | |
| | | | |
| | | | |
| | | | |
| | | | |
| | | | |
| | | | |
| | | | |
| | | | |
| | | | |
| | | | |
| | | | |
| | | | |

**EVENT:**

**LOCATION:**

**MAILING LIST**

**DATE:** **TIME:**

| NAME | EMAIL | PHONE | NOTE |
|------|-------|-------|------|
|      |       |       |      |
|      |       |       |      |
|      |       |       |      |
|      |       |       |      |
|      |       |       |      |
|      |       |       |      |
|      |       |       |      |
|      |       |       |      |
|      |       |       |      |
|      |       |       |      |
|      |       |       |      |
|      |       |       |      |
|      |       |       |      |
|      |       |       |      |
|      |       |       |      |
|      |       |       |      |
|      |       |       |      |
|      |       |       |      |
|      |       |       |      |
|      |       |       |      |
|      |       |       |      |
|      |       |       |      |
|      |       |       |      |
|      |       |       |      |

**EVENT:**

**LOCATION:**

**DATE:** **TIME:**

| NAME | EMAIL | PHONE | NOTE |
|------|-------|-------|------|
|      |       |       |      |
|      |       |       |      |
|      |       |       |      |
|      |       |       |      |
|      |       |       |      |
|      |       |       |      |
|      |       |       |      |
|      |       |       |      |
|      |       |       |      |
|      |       |       |      |
|      |       |       |      |
|      |       |       |      |
|      |       |       |      |
|      |       |       |      |
|      |       |       |      |
|      |       |       |      |
|      |       |       |      |
|      |       |       |      |
|      |       |       |      |
|      |       |       |      |
|      |       |       |      |
|      |       |       |      |
|      |       |       |      |
|      |       |       |      |

| EVENT: | | | MAILING LIST |
|--------|--|--|--------------|
| LOCATION: | | | DATE:     TIME: |

| NAME | EMAIL | PHONE | NOTE |
|------|-------|-------|------|
|  |  |  |  |
|  |  |  |  |
|  |  |  |  |
|  |  |  |  |
|  |  |  |  |
|  |  |  |  |
|  |  |  |  |
|  |  |  |  |
|  |  |  |  |
|  |  |  |  |
|  |  |  |  |
|  |  |  |  |
|  |  |  |  |
|  |  |  |  |
|  |  |  |  |
|  |  |  |  |
|  |  |  |  |
|  |  |  |  |
|  |  |  |  |
|  |  |  |  |
|  |  |  |  |
|  |  |  |  |
|  |  |  |  |

| EVENT: | | | MAILING LIST |
| LOCATION: | | | DATE:    TIME: |

| NAME | EMAIL | PHONE | NOTE |
| --- | --- | --- | --- |
| | | | |
| | | | |
| | | | |
| | | | |
| | | | |
| | | | |
| | | | |
| | | | |
| | | | |
| | | | |
| | | | |
| | | | |
| | | | |
| | | | |
| | | | |
| | | | |
| | | | |
| | | | |
| | | | |
| | | | |
| | | | |
| | | | |
| | | | |

**EVENT:**

**LOCATION:**

## MAILING LIST

**DATE:**  **TIME:**

| NAME | EMAIL | PHONE | NOTE |
|---|---|---|---|
| | | | |
| | | | |
| | | | |
| | | | |
| | | | |
| | | | |
| | | | |
| | | | |
| | | | |
| | | | |
| | | | |
| | | | |
| | | | |
| | | | |
| | | | |
| | | | |
| | | | |
| | | | |
| | | | |
| | | | |
| | | | |
| | | | |
| | | | |

| EVENT: | | MAILING LIST | |
|--------|--|--------------|--|
| LOCATION: | | DATE: | TIME: |

| NAME | EMAIL | PHONE | NOTE |
|------|-------|-------|------|
| | | | |
| | | | |
| | | | |
| | | | |
| | | | |
| | | | |
| | | | |
| | | | |
| | | | |
| | | | |
| | | | |
| | | | |
| | | | |
| | | | |
| | | | |
| | | | |
| | | | |
| | | | |
| | | | |
| | | | |
| | | | |
| | | | |
| | | | |
| | | | |
| | | | |

| EVENT: | | | MAILING LIST |
|--------|--|--|--------------|
| **LOCATION:** | | | **DATE:    TIME:** |

| NAME | EMAIL | PHONE | NOTE |
|------|-------|-------|------|
|      |       |       |      |
|      |       |       |      |
|      |       |       |      |
|      |       |       |      |
|      |       |       |      |
|      |       |       |      |
|      |       |       |      |
|      |       |       |      |
|      |       |       |      |
|      |       |       |      |
|      |       |       |      |
|      |       |       |      |
|      |       |       |      |
|      |       |       |      |
|      |       |       |      |
|      |       |       |      |
|      |       |       |      |
|      |       |       |      |
|      |       |       |      |
|      |       |       |      |
|      |       |       |      |
|      |       |       |      |
|      |       |       |      |
|      |       |       |      |

| EVENT: | | | |
|---|---|---|---|

**MAILING LIST**

| LOCATION: | | DATE: | TIME: |
|---|---|---|---|

| NAME | EMAIL | PHONE | NOTE |
|---|---|---|---|
| | | | |
| | | | |
| | | | |
| | | | |
| | | | |
| | | | |
| | | | |
| | | | |
| | | | |
| | | | |
| | | | |
| | | | |
| | | | |
| | | | |
| | | | |
| | | | |
| | | | |
| | | | |
| | | | |
| | | | |
| | | | |
| | | | |
| | | | |
| | | | |

**EVENT:**

**LOCATION:**

**MAILING LIST**

**DATE:**    **TIME:**

| NAME | EMAIL | PHONE | NOTE |
|------|-------|-------|------|
|  |  |  |  |
|  |  |  |  |
|  |  |  |  |
|  |  |  |  |
|  |  |  |  |
|  |  |  |  |
|  |  |  |  |
|  |  |  |  |
|  |  |  |  |
|  |  |  |  |
|  |  |  |  |
|  |  |  |  |
|  |  |  |  |
|  |  |  |  |
|  |  |  |  |
|  |  |  |  |
|  |  |  |  |
|  |  |  |  |
|  |  |  |  |
|  |  |  |  |
|  |  |  |  |
|  |  |  |  |

| EVENT: | | | MAILING LIST |
|--------|--|--|--------------|

| LOCATION: | | DATE:  TIME: |
|-----------|--|--------------|

| NAME | EMAIL | PHONE | NOTE |
|------|-------|-------|------|
|      |       |       |      |
|      |       |       |      |
|      |       |       |      |
|      |       |       |      |
|      |       |       |      |
|      |       |       |      |
|      |       |       |      |
|      |       |       |      |
|      |       |       |      |
|      |       |       |      |
|      |       |       |      |
|      |       |       |      |
|      |       |       |      |
|      |       |       |      |
|      |       |       |      |
|      |       |       |      |
|      |       |       |      |
|      |       |       |      |
|      |       |       |      |
|      |       |       |      |
|      |       |       |      |
|      |       |       |      |
|      |       |       |      |
|      |       |       |      |

| EVENT: | | MAILING LIST | |
| --- | --- | --- | --- |
| LOCATION: | | DATE: | TIME: |

| NAME | EMAIL | PHONE | NOTE |
| --- | --- | --- | --- |
| | | | |
| | | | |
| | | | |
| | | | |
| | | | |
| | | | |
| | | | |
| | | | |
| | | | |
| | | | |
| | | | |
| | | | |
| | | | |
| | | | |
| | | | |
| | | | |
| | | | |
| | | | |
| | | | |
| | | | |
| | | | |
| | | | |
| | | | |
| | | | |

**EVENT:**

**MAILING LIST**

**LOCATION:**

**DATE:** **TIME:**

| NAME | EMAIL | PHONE | NOTE |
|------|-------|-------|------|
|      |       |       |      |
|      |       |       |      |
|      |       |       |      |
|      |       |       |      |
|      |       |       |      |
|      |       |       |      |
|      |       |       |      |
|      |       |       |      |
|      |       |       |      |
|      |       |       |      |
|      |       |       |      |
|      |       |       |      |
|      |       |       |      |
|      |       |       |      |
|      |       |       |      |
|      |       |       |      |
|      |       |       |      |
|      |       |       |      |
|      |       |       |      |
|      |       |       |      |
|      |       |       |      |
|      |       |       |      |
|      |       |       |      |
|      |       |       |      |
|      |       |       |      |

**EVENT:**

**LOCATION:**

**MAILING LIST**

**DATE:**     **TIME:**

| NAME | EMAIL | PHONE | NOTE |
|------|-------|-------|------|
| | | | |
| | | | |
| | | | |
| | | | |
| | | | |
| | | | |
| | | | |
| | | | |
| | | | |
| | | | |
| | | | |
| | | | |
| | | | |
| | | | |
| | | | |
| | | | |
| | | | |
| | | | |
| | | | |
| | | | |
| | | | |
| | | | |
| | | | |
| | | | |
| | | | |

| EVENT: | | | MAILING LIST |
| --- | --- | --- | --- |
| LOCATION: | | | DATE: TIME: |

| NAME | EMAIL | PHONE | NOTE |
| --- | --- | --- | --- |
| | | | |
| | | | |
| | | | |
| | | | |
| | | | |
| | | | |
| | | | |
| | | | |
| | | | |
| | | | |
| | | | |
| | | | |
| | | | |
| | | | |
| | | | |
| | | | |
| | | | |
| | | | |
| | | | |
| | | | |
| | | | |
| | | | |
| | | | |
| | | | |
| | | | |
| | | | |

| EVENT: | | MAILING LIST | |
|--------|--|--------------|--|
| LOCATION: | | DATE:    TIME: | |

| NAME | EMAIL | PHONE | NOTE |
|------|-------|-------|------|
|  |  |  |  |
|  |  |  |  |
|  |  |  |  |
|  |  |  |  |
|  |  |  |  |
|  |  |  |  |
|  |  |  |  |
|  |  |  |  |
|  |  |  |  |
|  |  |  |  |
|  |  |  |  |
|  |  |  |  |
|  |  |  |  |
|  |  |  |  |
|  |  |  |  |
|  |  |  |  |
|  |  |  |  |
|  |  |  |  |
|  |  |  |  |
|  |  |  |  |
|  |  |  |  |

| EVENT: | | | MAILING LIST |
|---|---|---|---|
| LOCATION: | | | DATE: TIME: |

| NAME | EMAIL | PHONE | NOTE |
|---|---|---|---|
| | | | |
| | | | |
| | | | |
| | | | |
| | | | |
| | | | |
| | | | |
| | | | |
| | | | |
| | | | |
| | | | |
| | | | |
| | | | |
| | | | |
| | | | |
| | | | |
| | | | |
| | | | |
| | | | |
| | | | |
| | | | |
| | | | |
| | | | |

**EVENT:**

**LOCATION:**

**MAILING LIST**

**DATE:** **TIME:**

| NAME | EMAIL | PHONE | NOTE |
|------|-------|-------|------|
|      |       |       |      |
|      |       |       |      |
|      |       |       |      |
|      |       |       |      |
|      |       |       |      |
|      |       |       |      |
|      |       |       |      |
|      |       |       |      |
|      |       |       |      |
|      |       |       |      |
|      |       |       |      |
|      |       |       |      |
|      |       |       |      |
|      |       |       |      |
|      |       |       |      |
|      |       |       |      |
|      |       |       |      |
|      |       |       |      |
|      |       |       |      |
|      |       |       |      |
|      |       |       |      |
|      |       |       |      |
|      |       |       |      |

| EVENT: | | MAILING LIST | |
|---|---|---|---|
| LOCATION: | | DATE: TIME: | |

| NAME | EMAIL | PHONE | NOTE |
|---|---|---|---|
| | | | |
| | | | |
| | | | |
| | | | |
| | | | |
| | | | |
| | | | |
| | | | |
| | | | |
| | | | |
| | | | |
| | | | |
| | | | |
| | | | |
| | | | |
| | | | |
| | | | |
| | | | |
| | | | |
| | | | |
| | | | |
| | | | |
| | | | |
| | | | |

**EVENT:**

**MAILING LIST**

**LOCATION:**

**DATE:**     **TIME:**

| NAME | EMAIL | PHONE | NOTE |
|------|-------|-------|------|
|  |  |  |  |
|  |  |  |  |
|  |  |  |  |
|  |  |  |  |
|  |  |  |  |
|  |  |  |  |
|  |  |  |  |
|  |  |  |  |
|  |  |  |  |
|  |  |  |  |
|  |  |  |  |
|  |  |  |  |
|  |  |  |  |
|  |  |  |  |
|  |  |  |  |
|  |  |  |  |
|  |  |  |  |
|  |  |  |  |
|  |  |  |  |
|  |  |  |  |
|  |  |  |  |
|  |  |  |  |
|  |  |  |  |

EVENT:

LOCATION:

DATE:     TIME:

| NAME | EMAIL | PHONE | NOTE |
|------|-------|-------|------|
|      |       |       |      |
|      |       |       |      |
|      |       |       |      |
|      |       |       |      |
|      |       |       |      |
|      |       |       |      |
|      |       |       |      |
|      |       |       |      |
|      |       |       |      |
|      |       |       |      |
|      |       |       |      |
|      |       |       |      |
|      |       |       |      |
|      |       |       |      |
|      |       |       |      |
|      |       |       |      |
|      |       |       |      |
|      |       |       |      |
|      |       |       |      |
|      |       |       |      |
|      |       |       |      |
|      |       |       |      |
|      |       |       |      |
|      |       |       |      |

EVENT:

LOCATION:

**MAILING LIST**

DATE:        TIME:

| NAME | EMAIL | PHONE | NOTE |
|------|-------|-------|------|
|  |  |  |  |
|  |  |  |  |
|  |  |  |  |
|  |  |  |  |
|  |  |  |  |
|  |  |  |  |
|  |  |  |  |
|  |  |  |  |
|  |  |  |  |
|  |  |  |  |
|  |  |  |  |
|  |  |  |  |
|  |  |  |  |
|  |  |  |  |
|  |  |  |  |
|  |  |  |  |
|  |  |  |  |
|  |  |  |  |
|  |  |  |  |
|  |  |  |  |
|  |  |  |  |
|  |  |  |  |
|  |  |  |  |
|  |  |  |  |

EVENT:

LOCATION:

DATE:    TIME:

| NAME | EMAIL | PHONE | NOTE |
|------|-------|-------|------|
|      |       |       |      |
|      |       |       |      |
|      |       |       |      |
|      |       |       |      |
|      |       |       |      |
|      |       |       |      |
|      |       |       |      |
|      |       |       |      |
|      |       |       |      |
|      |       |       |      |
|      |       |       |      |
|      |       |       |      |
|      |       |       |      |
|      |       |       |      |
|      |       |       |      |
|      |       |       |      |
|      |       |       |      |
|      |       |       |      |
|      |       |       |      |
|      |       |       |      |
|      |       |       |      |
|      |       |       |      |
|      |       |       |      |
|      |       |       |      |

| EVENT: | | MAILING LIST | |
| --- | --- | --- | --- |
| LOCATION: | | DATE:    TIME: | |

| NAME | EMAIL | PHONE | NOTE |
| --- | --- | --- | --- |
| | | | |
| | | | |
| | | | |
| | | | |
| | | | |
| | | | |
| | | | |
| | | | |
| | | | |
| | | | |
| | | | |
| | | | |
| | | | |
| | | | |
| | | | |
| | | | |
| | | | |
| | | | |
| | | | |
| | | | |
| | | | |
| | | | |

**EVENT:**

**LOCATION:**

## MAILING LIST

**DATE:**    **TIME:**

| NAME | EMAIL | PHONE | NOTE |
|------|-------|-------|------|
|      |       |       |      |
|      |       |       |      |
|      |       |       |      |
|      |       |       |      |
|      |       |       |      |
|      |       |       |      |
|      |       |       |      |
|      |       |       |      |
|      |       |       |      |
|      |       |       |      |
|      |       |       |      |
|      |       |       |      |
|      |       |       |      |
|      |       |       |      |
|      |       |       |      |
|      |       |       |      |
|      |       |       |      |
|      |       |       |      |
|      |       |       |      |
|      |       |       |      |
|      |       |       |      |
|      |       |       |      |
|      |       |       |      |
|      |       |       |      |

**EVENT:**

**LOCATION:**

## MAILING LIST

**DATE:**     **TIME:**

| NAME | EMAIL | PHONE | NOTE |
|---|---|---|---|
| | | | |
| | | | |
| | | | |
| | | | |
| | | | |
| | | | |
| | | | |
| | | | |
| | | | |
| | | | |
| | | | |
| | | | |
| | | | |
| | | | |
| | | | |
| | | | |
| | | | |
| | | | |
| | | | |
| | | | |
| | | | |
| | | | |
| | | | |
| | | | |

| EVENT: | | MAILING LIST | |
|---|---|---|---|
| LOCATION: | | DATE: TIME: | |

| NAME | EMAIL | PHONE | NOTE |
|---|---|---|---|
| | | | |
| | | | |
| | | | |
| | | | |
| | | | |
| | | | |
| | | | |
| | | | |
| | | | |
| | | | |
| | | | |
| | | | |
| | | | |
| | | | |
| | | | |
| | | | |
| | | | |
| | | | |
| | | | |
| | | | |
| | | | |
| | | | |

**EVENT:**

**LOCATION:**

**MAILING LIST**

**DATE:**     **TIME:**

| NAME | EMAIL | PHONE | NOTE |
|------|-------|-------|------|
|  |  |  |  |
|  |  |  |  |
|  |  |  |  |
|  |  |  |  |
|  |  |  |  |
|  |  |  |  |
|  |  |  |  |
|  |  |  |  |
|  |  |  |  |
|  |  |  |  |
|  |  |  |  |
|  |  |  |  |
|  |  |  |  |
|  |  |  |  |
|  |  |  |  |
|  |  |  |  |
|  |  |  |  |
|  |  |  |  |
|  |  |  |  |
|  |  |  |  |
|  |  |  |  |
|  |  |  |  |

| EVENT: | | | |
| --- | --- | --- | --- |
| LOCATION: | | DATE: | TIME: |

**MAILING LIST**

| NAME | EMAIL | PHONE | NOTE |
| --- | --- | --- | --- |
| | | | |
| | | | |
| | | | |
| | | | |
| | | | |
| | | | |
| | | | |
| | | | |
| | | | |
| | | | |
| | | | |
| | | | |
| | | | |
| | | | |
| | | | |
| | | | |
| | | | |
| | | | |
| | | | |
| | | | |
| | | | |
| | | | |
| | | | |
| | | | |

| EVENT: | | MAILING LIST | |
|---|---|---|---|
| LOCATION: | | DATE: | TIME: |

| NAME | EMAIL | PHONE | NOTE |
|---|---|---|---|
| | | | |
| | | | |
| | | | |
| | | | |
| | | | |
| | | | |
| | | | |
| | | | |
| | | | |
| | | | |
| | | | |
| | | | |
| | | | |
| | | | |
| | | | |
| | | | |
| | | | |
| | | | |
| | | | |
| | | | |
| | | | |
| | | | |
| | | | |
| | | | |
| | | | |
| | | | |
| | | | |

| EVENT: | | | MAILING LIST |
|---|---|---|---|
| LOCATION: | | | DATE:    TIME: |

| NAME | EMAIL | PHONE | NOTE |
|---|---|---|---|
| | | | |
| | | | |
| | | | |
| | | | |
| | | | |
| | | | |
| | | | |
| | | | |
| | | | |
| | | | |
| | | | |
| | | | |
| | | | |
| | | | |
| | | | |
| | | | |
| | | | |
| | | | |
| | | | |
| | | | |
| | | | |
| | | | |
| | | | |
| | | | |
| | | | |
| | | | |

| EVENT: | | | MAILING LIST |
|--------|--|--|--------------|
| LOCATION: | | | DATE:     TIME: |

| NAME | EMAIL | PHONE | NOTE |
|------|-------|-------|------|
|      |       |       |      |
|      |       |       |      |
|      |       |       |      |
|      |       |       |      |
|      |       |       |      |
|      |       |       |      |
|      |       |       |      |
|      |       |       |      |
|      |       |       |      |
|      |       |       |      |
|      |       |       |      |
|      |       |       |      |
|      |       |       |      |
|      |       |       |      |
|      |       |       |      |
|      |       |       |      |
|      |       |       |      |
|      |       |       |      |
|      |       |       |      |
|      |       |       |      |
|      |       |       |      |
|      |       |       |      |
|      |       |       |      |
|      |       |       |      |
|      |       |       |      |

**EVENT:**

**LOCATION:**

## MAILING LIST

**DATE:**  **TIME:**

| NAME | EMAIL | PHONE | NOTE |
|------|-------|-------|------|
|      |       |       |      |
|      |       |       |      |
|      |       |       |      |
|      |       |       |      |
|      |       |       |      |
|      |       |       |      |
|      |       |       |      |
|      |       |       |      |
|      |       |       |      |
|      |       |       |      |
|      |       |       |      |
|      |       |       |      |
|      |       |       |      |
|      |       |       |      |
|      |       |       |      |
|      |       |       |      |
|      |       |       |      |
|      |       |       |      |
|      |       |       |      |
|      |       |       |      |
|      |       |       |      |
|      |       |       |      |
|      |       |       |      |
|      |       |       |      |

| EVENT: | | | **MAILING LIST** |
|---|---|---|---|
| LOCATION: | | | DATE:    TIME: |

| NAME | EMAIL | PHONE | NOTE |
|---|---|---|---|
|  |  |  |  |
|  |  |  |  |
|  |  |  |  |
|  |  |  |  |
|  |  |  |  |
|  |  |  |  |
|  |  |  |  |
|  |  |  |  |
|  |  |  |  |
|  |  |  |  |
|  |  |  |  |
|  |  |  |  |
|  |  |  |  |
|  |  |  |  |
|  |  |  |  |
|  |  |  |  |
|  |  |  |  |
|  |  |  |  |
|  |  |  |  |
|  |  |  |  |
|  |  |  |  |
|  |  |  |  |
|  |  |  |  |
|  |  |  |  |
|  |  |  |  |
|  |  |  |  |

## MAILING LIST

**EVENT:**

**LOCATION:**

**DATE:**  **TIME:**

| NAME | EMAIL | PHONE | NOTE |
|------|-------|-------|------|
|  |  |  |  |
|  |  |  |  |
|  |  |  |  |
|  |  |  |  |
|  |  |  |  |
|  |  |  |  |
|  |  |  |  |
|  |  |  |  |
|  |  |  |  |
|  |  |  |  |
|  |  |  |  |
|  |  |  |  |
|  |  |  |  |
|  |  |  |  |
|  |  |  |  |
|  |  |  |  |
|  |  |  |  |
|  |  |  |  |
|  |  |  |  |
|  |  |  |  |
|  |  |  |  |
|  |  |  |  |
|  |  |  |  |
|  |  |  |  |
|  |  |  |  |

| EVENT: | | | MAILING LIST |
| --- | --- | --- | --- |
| LOCATION: | | | DATE:    TIME: |

| NAME | EMAIL | PHONE | NOTE |
| --- | --- | --- | --- |
| | | | |
| | | | |
| | | | |
| | | | |
| | | | |
| | | | |
| | | | |
| | | | |
| | | | |
| | | | |
| | | | |
| | | | |
| | | | |
| | | | |
| | | | |
| | | | |
| | | | |
| | | | |
| | | | |
| | | | |
| | | | |
| | | | |
| | | | |

| EVENT: | | | MAILING LIST |
|---|---|---|---|
| LOCATION: | | | DATE:   TIME: |

| NAME | EMAIL | PHONE | NOTE |
|---|---|---|---|
| | | | |
| | | | |
| | | | |
| | | | |
| | | | |
| | | | |
| | | | |
| | | | |
| | | | |
| | | | |
| | | | |
| | | | |
| | | | |
| | | | |
| | | | |
| | | | |
| | | | |
| | | | |
| | | | |
| | | | |
| | | | |
| | | | |
| | | | |
| | | | |

| EVENT: | | | MAILING LIST |
| --- | --- | --- | --- |
| LOCATION: | | | DATE:      TIME: |

| NAME | EMAIL | PHONE | NOTE |
| --- | --- | --- | --- |
| | | | |
| | | | |
| | | | |
| | | | |
| | | | |
| | | | |
| | | | |
| | | | |
| | | | |
| | | | |
| | | | |
| | | | |
| | | | |
| | | | |
| | | | |
| | | | |
| | | | |
| | | | |
| | | | |
| | | | |
| | | | |
| | | | |
| | | | |
| | | | |
| | | | |

| EVENT: | | MAILING LIST | |
|---|---|---|---|
| LOCATION: | | DATE: | TIME: |

| NAME | EMAIL | PHONE | NOTE |
|---|---|---|---|
| | | | |
| | | | |
| | | | |
| | | | |
| | | | |
| | | | |
| | | | |
| | | | |
| | | | |
| | | | |
| | | | |
| | | | |
| | | | |
| | | | |
| | | | |
| | | | |
| | | | |
| | | | |
| | | | |
| | | | |
| | | | |
| | | | |
| | | | |
| | | | |
| | | | |
| | | | |
| | | | |

**EVENT:**

**LOCATION:**

**MAILING LIST**

**DATE:**     **TIME:**

| NAME | EMAIL | PHONE | NOTE |
|------|-------|-------|------|
|      |       |       |      |
|      |       |       |      |
|      |       |       |      |
|      |       |       |      |
|      |       |       |      |
|      |       |       |      |
|      |       |       |      |
|      |       |       |      |
|      |       |       |      |
|      |       |       |      |
|      |       |       |      |
|      |       |       |      |
|      |       |       |      |
|      |       |       |      |
|      |       |       |      |
|      |       |       |      |
|      |       |       |      |
|      |       |       |      |
|      |       |       |      |
|      |       |       |      |

**EVENT:**

**LOCATION:**

**MAILING LIST**

**DATE:**   **TIME:**

| NAME | EMAIL | PHONE | NOTE |
|------|-------|-------|------|
|      |       |       |      |
|      |       |       |      |
|      |       |       |      |
|      |       |       |      |
|      |       |       |      |
|      |       |       |      |
|      |       |       |      |
|      |       |       |      |
|      |       |       |      |
|      |       |       |      |
|      |       |       |      |
|      |       |       |      |
|      |       |       |      |
|      |       |       |      |
|      |       |       |      |
|      |       |       |      |
|      |       |       |      |
|      |       |       |      |
|      |       |       |      |
|      |       |       |      |
|      |       |       |      |
|      |       |       |      |

EVENT:

## MAILING LIST

LOCATION:

DATE:     TIME:

| NAME | EMAIL | PHONE | NOTE |
|------|-------|-------|------|
|      |       |       |      |
|      |       |       |      |
|      |       |       |      |
|      |       |       |      |
|      |       |       |      |
|      |       |       |      |
|      |       |       |      |
|      |       |       |      |
|      |       |       |      |
|      |       |       |      |
|      |       |       |      |
|      |       |       |      |
|      |       |       |      |
|      |       |       |      |
|      |       |       |      |
|      |       |       |      |
|      |       |       |      |
|      |       |       |      |
|      |       |       |      |
|      |       |       |      |
|      |       |       |      |
|      |       |       |      |
|      |       |       |      |
|      |       |       |      |
|      |       |       |      |

| EVENT: |  |  | **MAILING LIST** |
|---|---|---|---|
| LOCATION: |  | DATE: | TIME: |

| NAME | EMAIL | PHONE | NOTE |
|---|---|---|---|
|  |  |  |  |
|  |  |  |  |
|  |  |  |  |
|  |  |  |  |
|  |  |  |  |
|  |  |  |  |
|  |  |  |  |
|  |  |  |  |
|  |  |  |  |
|  |  |  |  |
|  |  |  |  |
|  |  |  |  |
|  |  |  |  |
|  |  |  |  |
|  |  |  |  |
|  |  |  |  |
|  |  |  |  |
|  |  |  |  |
|  |  |  |  |
|  |  |  |  |
|  |  |  |  |
|  |  |  |  |
|  |  |  |  |
|  |  |  |  |
|  |  |  |  |

| EVENT: | | MAILING LIST | |
|---|---|---|---|
| LOCATION: | | DATE: TIME: | |

| NAME | EMAIL | PHONE | NOTE |
|---|---|---|---|
| | | | |
| | | | |
| | | | |
| | | | |
| | | | |
| | | | |
| | | | |
| | | | |
| | | | |
| | | | |
| | | | |
| | | | |
| | | | |
| | | | |
| | | | |
| | | | |
| | | | |
| | | | |
| | | | |
| | | | |
| | | | |
| | | | |
| | | | |
| | | | |

**EVENT:**

**LOCATION:**

## MAILING LIST

**DATE:**   **TIME:**

| NAME | EMAIL | PHONE | NOTE |
|------|-------|-------|------|
|  |  |  |  |
|  |  |  |  |
|  |  |  |  |
|  |  |  |  |
|  |  |  |  |
|  |  |  |  |
|  |  |  |  |
|  |  |  |  |
|  |  |  |  |
|  |  |  |  |
|  |  |  |  |
|  |  |  |  |
|  |  |  |  |
|  |  |  |  |
|  |  |  |  |
|  |  |  |  |
|  |  |  |  |
|  |  |  |  |
|  |  |  |  |
|  |  |  |  |
|  |  |  |  |
|  |  |  |  |
|  |  |  |  |
|  |  |  |  |

| EVENT: | | MAILING LIST | |
|---|---|---|---|
| LOCATION: | | DATE: | TIME: |

| NAME | EMAIL | PHONE | NOTE |
|---|---|---|---|
| | | | |
| | | | |
| | | | |
| | | | |
| | | | |
| | | | |
| | | | |
| | | | |
| | | | |
| | | | |
| | | | |
| | | | |
| | | | |
| | | | |
| | | | |
| | | | |
| | | | |
| | | | |
| | | | |
| | | | |
| | | | |
| | | | |
| | | | |
| | | | |
| | | | |

| EVENT: | | | | MAILING LIST |
|--------|--|--|--|--------------|

| LOCATION: | | | DATE: | TIME: |
|-----------|--|--|-------|-------|

| NAME | EMAIL | PHONE | NOTE |
|------|-------|-------|------|
|  |  |  |  |
|  |  |  |  |
|  |  |  |  |
|  |  |  |  |
|  |  |  |  |
|  |  |  |  |
|  |  |  |  |
|  |  |  |  |
|  |  |  |  |
|  |  |  |  |
|  |  |  |  |
|  |  |  |  |
|  |  |  |  |
|  |  |  |  |
|  |  |  |  |
|  |  |  |  |
|  |  |  |  |
|  |  |  |  |
|  |  |  |  |
|  |  |  |  |
|  |  |  |  |
|  |  |  |  |
|  |  |  |  |
|  |  |  |  |
|  |  |  |  |

| EVENT: | | | MAILING LIST |
|---|---|---|---|
| **LOCATION:** | | | **DATE:      TIME:** |

| NAME | EMAIL | PHONE | NOTE |
|---|---|---|---|
| | | | |
| | | | |
| | | | |
| | | | |
| | | | |
| | | | |
| | | | |
| | | | |
| | | | |
| | | | |
| | | | |
| | | | |
| | | | |
| | | | |
| | | | |
| | | | |
| | | | |
| | | | |
| | | | |
| | | | |
| | | | |
| | | | |
| | | | |

## MAILING LIST

| EVENT: |
|---|

| LOCATION: |
|---|

| DATE: | TIME: |
|---|---|

| NAME | EMAIL | PHONE | NOTE |
|---|---|---|---|
| | | | |
| | | | |
| | | | |
| | | | |
| | | | |
| | | | |
| | | | |
| | | | |
| | | | |
| | | | |
| | | | |
| | | | |
| | | | |
| | | | |
| | | | |
| | | | |
| | | | |
| | | | |
| | | | |
| | | | |
| | | | |
| | | | |
| | | | |
| | | | |
| | | | |

**EVENT:**

**LOCATION:**

**MAILING LIST**

**DATE:**     **TIME:**

| NAME | EMAIL | PHONE | NOTE |
|------|-------|-------|------|
|  |  |  |  |
|  |  |  |  |
|  |  |  |  |
|  |  |  |  |
|  |  |  |  |
|  |  |  |  |
|  |  |  |  |
|  |  |  |  |
|  |  |  |  |
|  |  |  |  |
|  |  |  |  |
|  |  |  |  |
|  |  |  |  |
|  |  |  |  |
|  |  |  |  |
|  |  |  |  |
|  |  |  |  |
|  |  |  |  |
|  |  |  |  |
|  |  |  |  |
|  |  |  |  |
|  |  |  |  |
|  |  |  |  |
|  |  |  |  |
|  |  |  |  |

**EVENT:**

**LOCATION:**

**MAILING LIST**

**DATE:** **TIME:**

| NAME | EMAIL | PHONE | NOTE |
|------|-------|-------|------|
|  |  |  |  |
|  |  |  |  |
|  |  |  |  |
|  |  |  |  |
|  |  |  |  |
|  |  |  |  |
|  |  |  |  |
|  |  |  |  |
|  |  |  |  |
|  |  |  |  |
|  |  |  |  |
|  |  |  |  |
|  |  |  |  |
|  |  |  |  |
|  |  |  |  |
|  |  |  |  |
|  |  |  |  |
|  |  |  |  |
|  |  |  |  |
|  |  |  |  |
|  |  |  |  |
|  |  |  |  |
|  |  |  |  |
|  |  |  |  |
|  |  |  |  |

| EVENT: | | | MAILING LIST |
| LOCATION: | | | DATE:     TIME: |

| NAME | EMAIL | PHONE | NOTE |
|------|-------|-------|------|
|  |  |  |  |
|  |  |  |  |
|  |  |  |  |
|  |  |  |  |
|  |  |  |  |
|  |  |  |  |
|  |  |  |  |
|  |  |  |  |
|  |  |  |  |
|  |  |  |  |
|  |  |  |  |
|  |  |  |  |
|  |  |  |  |
|  |  |  |  |
|  |  |  |  |
|  |  |  |  |
|  |  |  |  |
|  |  |  |  |
|  |  |  |  |
|  |  |  |  |
|  |  |  |  |
|  |  |  |  |
|  |  |  |  |
|  |  |  |  |

**EVENT:**

**LOCATION:**

**MAILING LIST**

**DATE:**    **TIME:**

| NAME | EMAIL | PHONE | NOTE |
|------|-------|-------|------|
|      |       |       |      |
|      |       |       |      |
|      |       |       |      |
|      |       |       |      |
|      |       |       |      |
|      |       |       |      |
|      |       |       |      |
|      |       |       |      |
|      |       |       |      |
|      |       |       |      |
|      |       |       |      |
|      |       |       |      |
|      |       |       |      |
|      |       |       |      |
|      |       |       |      |
|      |       |       |      |
|      |       |       |      |
|      |       |       |      |
|      |       |       |      |
|      |       |       |      |
|      |       |       |      |

**EVENT:**

**LOCATION:**

**MAILING LIST**

**DATE:**     **TIME:**

| NAME | EMAIL | PHONE | NOTE |
|------|-------|-------|------|
|  |  |  |  |
|  |  |  |  |
|  |  |  |  |
|  |  |  |  |
|  |  |  |  |
|  |  |  |  |
|  |  |  |  |
|  |  |  |  |
|  |  |  |  |
|  |  |  |  |
|  |  |  |  |
|  |  |  |  |
|  |  |  |  |
|  |  |  |  |
|  |  |  |  |
|  |  |  |  |
|  |  |  |  |
|  |  |  |  |
|  |  |  |  |
|  |  |  |  |
|  |  |  |  |
|  |  |  |  |
|  |  |  |  |
|  |  |  |  |
|  |  |  |  |

| EVENT: | | | MAILING LIST |
| --- | --- | --- | --- |
| LOCATION: | | | DATE:    TIME: |

| NAME | EMAIL | PHONE | NOTE |
| --- | --- | --- | --- |
| | | | |
| | | | |
| | | | |
| | | | |
| | | | |
| | | | |
| | | | |
| | | | |
| | | | |
| | | | |
| | | | |
| | | | |
| | | | |
| | | | |
| | | | |
| | | | |
| | | | |
| | | | |
| | | | |
| | | | |
| | | | |
| | | | |
| | | | |

| EVENT: | | | MAILING LIST |
| --- | --- | --- | --- |
| LOCATION: | | | DATE:    TIME: |

| NAME | EMAIL | PHONE | NOTE |
| --- | --- | --- | --- |
| | | | |
| | | | |
| | | | |
| | | | |
| | | | |
| | | | |
| | | | |
| | | | |
| | | | |
| | | | |
| | | | |
| | | | |
| | | | |
| | | | |
| | | | |
| | | | |
| | | | |
| | | | |
| | | | |
| | | | |
| | | | |
| | | | |
| | | | |
| | | | |
| | | | |

**EVENT:**

**LOCATION:**

**MAILING LIST**

**DATE:**  **TIME:**

| NAME | EMAIL | PHONE | NOTE |
|------|-------|-------|------|
|      |       |       |      |
|      |       |       |      |
|      |       |       |      |
|      |       |       |      |
|      |       |       |      |
|      |       |       |      |
|      |       |       |      |
|      |       |       |      |
|      |       |       |      |
|      |       |       |      |
|      |       |       |      |
|      |       |       |      |
|      |       |       |      |
|      |       |       |      |
|      |       |       |      |
|      |       |       |      |
|      |       |       |      |
|      |       |       |      |
|      |       |       |      |
|      |       |       |      |
|      |       |       |      |
|      |       |       |      |
|      |       |       |      |

| EVENT: | | MAILING LIST | |
|--------|--|--------------|--|
| LOCATION: | | DATE: | TIME: |

| NAME | EMAIL | PHONE | NOTE |
|------|-------|-------|------|
| | | | |
| | | | |
| | | | |
| | | | |
| | | | |
| | | | |
| | | | |
| | | | |
| | | | |
| | | | |
| | | | |
| | | | |
| | | | |
| | | | |
| | | | |
| | | | |
| | | | |
| | | | |
| | | | |
| | | | |
| | | | |
| | | | |
| | | | |
| | | | |
| | | | |
| | | | |

| EVENT: | | | MAILING LIST |
| LOCATION: | | | DATE: TIME: |

| NAME | EMAIL | PHONE | NOTE |
|---|---|---|---|
| | | | |
| | | | |
| | | | |
| | | | |
| | | | |
| | | | |
| | | | |
| | | | |
| | | | |
| | | | |
| | | | |
| | | | |
| | | | |
| | | | |
| | | | |
| | | | |
| | | | |
| | | | |
| | | | |
| | | | |
| | | | |
| | | | |
| | | | |
| | | | |
| | | | |

| EVENT: | | | MAILING LIST |
|---|---|---|---|
| **LOCATION:** | | | **DATE:** **TIME:** |

| NAME | EMAIL | PHONE | NOTE |
|---|---|---|---|
|  |  |  |  |
|  |  |  |  |
|  |  |  |  |
|  |  |  |  |
|  |  |  |  |
|  |  |  |  |
|  |  |  |  |
|  |  |  |  |
|  |  |  |  |
|  |  |  |  |
|  |  |  |  |
|  |  |  |  |
|  |  |  |  |
|  |  |  |  |
|  |  |  |  |
|  |  |  |  |
|  |  |  |  |
|  |  |  |  |
|  |  |  |  |
|  |  |  |  |
|  |  |  |  |
|  |  |  |  |

**EVENT:**

**LOCATION:**

**DATE:**     **TIME:**

| NAME | EMAIL | PHONE | NOTE |
|------|-------|-------|------|
|      |       |       |      |
|      |       |       |      |
|      |       |       |      |
|      |       |       |      |
|      |       |       |      |
|      |       |       |      |
|      |       |       |      |
|      |       |       |      |
|      |       |       |      |
|      |       |       |      |
|      |       |       |      |
|      |       |       |      |
|      |       |       |      |
|      |       |       |      |
|      |       |       |      |
|      |       |       |      |
|      |       |       |      |
|      |       |       |      |
|      |       |       |      |
|      |       |       |      |
|      |       |       |      |
|      |       |       |      |
|      |       |       |      |
|      |       |       |      |
|      |       |       |      |

**EVENT:**

**LOCATION:**

## MAILING LIST

**DATE:**    **TIME:**

| NAME | EMAIL | PHONE | NOTE |
|------|-------|-------|------|
|      |       |       |      |
|      |       |       |      |
|      |       |       |      |
|      |       |       |      |
|      |       |       |      |
|      |       |       |      |
|      |       |       |      |
|      |       |       |      |
|      |       |       |      |
|      |       |       |      |
|      |       |       |      |
|      |       |       |      |
|      |       |       |      |
|      |       |       |      |
|      |       |       |      |
|      |       |       |      |
|      |       |       |      |
|      |       |       |      |
|      |       |       |      |
|      |       |       |      |
|      |       |       |      |
|      |       |       |      |
|      |       |       |      |

**EVENT:**

**LOCATION:**

## MAILING LIST

**DATE:**    **TIME:**

| NAME | EMAIL | PHONE | NOTE |
|------|-------|-------|------|
|      |       |       |      |
|      |       |       |      |
|      |       |       |      |
|      |       |       |      |
|      |       |       |      |
|      |       |       |      |
|      |       |       |      |
|      |       |       |      |
|      |       |       |      |
|      |       |       |      |
|      |       |       |      |
|      |       |       |      |
|      |       |       |      |
|      |       |       |      |
|      |       |       |      |
|      |       |       |      |
|      |       |       |      |
|      |       |       |      |
|      |       |       |      |
|      |       |       |      |
|      |       |       |      |
|      |       |       |      |
|      |       |       |      |
|      |       |       |      |

| EVENT: | | MAILING LIST | |
|---|---|---|---|
| LOCATION: | | DATE: TIME: | |

| NAME | EMAIL | PHONE | NOTE |
|---|---|---|---|
| | | | |
| | | | |
| | | | |
| | | | |
| | | | |
| | | | |
| | | | |
| | | | |
| | | | |
| | | | |
| | | | |
| | | | |
| | | | |
| | | | |
| | | | |
| | | | |
| | | | |
| | | | |
| | | | |
| | | | |
| | | | |
| | | | |
| | | | |
| | | | |

| EVENT: | | MAILING LIST | |
|---|---|---|---|
| LOCATION: | | DATE: | TIME: |

| NAME | EMAIL | PHONE | NOTE |
|---|---|---|---|
| | | | |
| | | | |
| | | | |
| | | | |
| | | | |
| | | | |
| | | | |
| | | | |
| | | | |
| | | | |
| | | | |
| | | | |
| | | | |
| | | | |
| | | | |
| | | | |
| | | | |
| | | | |
| | | | |
| | | | |
| | | | |
| | | | |
| | | | |
| | | | |

| EVENT: | | | MAILING LIST |
| LOCATION: | | | DATE:     TIME: |

| NAME | EMAIL | PHONE | NOTE |
| --- | --- | --- | --- |
|  |  |  |  |
|  |  |  |  |
|  |  |  |  |
|  |  |  |  |
|  |  |  |  |
|  |  |  |  |
|  |  |  |  |
|  |  |  |  |
|  |  |  |  |
|  |  |  |  |
|  |  |  |  |
|  |  |  |  |
|  |  |  |  |
|  |  |  |  |
|  |  |  |  |
|  |  |  |  |
|  |  |  |  |
|  |  |  |  |
|  |  |  |  |
|  |  |  |  |
|  |  |  |  |
|  |  |  |  |
|  |  |  |  |

| EVENT: | | | |
|---|---|---|---|

**MAILING LIST**

| LOCATION: | | DATE: | TIME: |
|---|---|---|---|

| NAME | EMAIL | PHONE | NOTE |
|---|---|---|---|
| | | | |
| | | | |
| | | | |
| | | | |
| | | | |
| | | | |
| | | | |
| | | | |
| | | | |
| | | | |
| | | | |
| | | | |
| | | | |
| | | | |
| | | | |
| | | | |
| | | | |
| | | | |
| | | | |
| | | | |
| | | | |
| | | | |
| | | | |
| | | | |
| | | | |

# MAILING LIST

**EVENT:**

**LOCATION:**

**DATE:**    **TIME:**

| NAME | EMAIL | PHONE | NOTE |
|------|-------|-------|------|
|      |       |       |      |
|      |       |       |      |
|      |       |       |      |
|      |       |       |      |
|      |       |       |      |
|      |       |       |      |
|      |       |       |      |
|      |       |       |      |
|      |       |       |      |
|      |       |       |      |
|      |       |       |      |
|      |       |       |      |
|      |       |       |      |
|      |       |       |      |
|      |       |       |      |
|      |       |       |      |
|      |       |       |      |
|      |       |       |      |
|      |       |       |      |
|      |       |       |      |
|      |       |       |      |
|      |       |       |      |

**EVENT:**

**LOCATION:**

**MAILING LIST**

**DATE:**     **TIME:**

| NAME | EMAIL | PHONE | NOTE |
|------|-------|-------|------|
| | | | |
| | | | |
| | | | |
| | | | |
| | | | |
| | | | |
| | | | |
| | | | |
| | | | |
| | | | |
| | | | |
| | | | |
| | | | |
| | | | |
| | | | |
| | | | |
| | | | |
| | | | |
| | | | |
| | | | |
| | | | |
| | | | |
| | | | |

| EVENT: | | | |
|---|---|---|---|
| **LOCATION:** | | | |

| | | DATE: | TIME: |
|---|---|---|---|

| NAME | EMAIL | PHONE | NOTE |
|---|---|---|---|
| | | | |
| | | | |
| | | | |
| | | | |
| | | | |
| | | | |
| | | | |
| | | | |
| | | | |
| | | | |
| | | | |
| | | | |
| | | | |
| | | | |
| | | | |
| | | | |
| | | | |
| | | | |
| | | | |
| | | | |
| | | | |
| | | | |
| | | | |
| | | | |

| EVENT: | | | |
|---|---|---|---|

| LOCATION: | | DATE: | TIME: |
|---|---|---|---|

| NAME | EMAIL | PHONE | NOTE |
|---|---|---|---|
| | | | |
| | | | |
| | | | |
| | | | |
| | | | |
| | | | |
| | | | |
| | | | |
| | | | |
| | | | |
| | | | |
| | | | |
| | | | |
| | | | |
| | | | |
| | | | |
| | | | |
| | | | |
| | | | |
| | | | |
| | | | |
| | | | |
| | | | |
| | | | |
| | | | |

**EVENT:**

**LOCATION:**

**MAILING LIST**

**DATE:**   **TIME:**

| NAME | EMAIL | PHONE | NOTE |
|------|-------|-------|------|
|  |  |  |  |
|  |  |  |  |
|  |  |  |  |
|  |  |  |  |
|  |  |  |  |
|  |  |  |  |
|  |  |  |  |
|  |  |  |  |
|  |  |  |  |
|  |  |  |  |
|  |  |  |  |
|  |  |  |  |
|  |  |  |  |
|  |  |  |  |
|  |  |  |  |
|  |  |  |  |
|  |  |  |  |
|  |  |  |  |
|  |  |  |  |
|  |  |  |  |
|  |  |  |  |
|  |  |  |  |

| EVENT: | | | |
|---|---|---|---|

**MAILING LIST**

| LOCATION: | | DATE: | TIME: |
|---|---|---|---|

| NAME | EMAIL | PHONE | NOTE |
|---|---|---|---|
| | | | |
| | | | |
| | | | |
| | | | |
| | | | |
| | | | |
| | | | |
| | | | |
| | | | |
| | | | |
| | | | |
| | | | |
| | | | |
| | | | |
| | | | |
| | | | |
| | | | |
| | | | |
| | | | |
| | | | |
| | | | |
| | | | |
| | | | |

**EVENT:**

**LOCATION:**

**MAILING LIST**

**DATE:**     **TIME:**

| NAME | EMAIL | PHONE | NOTE |
|------|-------|-------|------|
|      |       |       |      |
|      |       |       |      |
|      |       |       |      |
|      |       |       |      |
|      |       |       |      |
|      |       |       |      |
|      |       |       |      |
|      |       |       |      |
|      |       |       |      |
|      |       |       |      |
|      |       |       |      |
|      |       |       |      |
|      |       |       |      |
|      |       |       |      |
|      |       |       |      |
|      |       |       |      |
|      |       |       |      |
|      |       |       |      |
|      |       |       |      |
|      |       |       |      |
|      |       |       |      |
|      |       |       |      |
|      |       |       |      |
|      |       |       |      |

| EVENT: | | | MAILING LIST |
|---|---|---|---|
| LOCATION: | | | DATE:    TIME: |

| NAME | EMAIL | PHONE | NOTE |
|---|---|---|---|
| | | | |
| | | | |
| | | | |
| | | | |
| | | | |
| | | | |
| | | | |
| | | | |
| | | | |
| | | | |
| | | | |
| | | | |
| | | | |
| | | | |
| | | | |
| | | | |
| | | | |
| | | | |
| | | | |
| | | | |
| | | | |
| | | | |
| | | | |

| EVENT: | | MAILING LIST | |
|---|---|---|---|
| LOCATION: | | DATE: TIME: | |

| NAME | EMAIL | PHONE | NOTE |
|---|---|---|---|
| | | | |
| | | | |
| | | | |
| | | | |
| | | | |
| | | | |
| | | | |
| | | | |
| | | | |
| | | | |
| | | | |
| | | | |
| | | | |
| | | | |
| | | | |
| | | | |
| | | | |
| | | | |
| | | | |
| | | | |
| | | | |
| | | | |
| | | | |
| | | | |

| EVENT: | | | MAILING LIST |
|---|---|---|---|

| LOCATION: | | DATE: | TIME: |
|---|---|---|---|

| NAME | EMAIL | PHONE | NOTE |
|---|---|---|---|
| | | | |
| | | | |
| | | | |
| | | | |
| | | | |
| | | | |
| | | | |
| | | | |
| | | | |
| | | | |
| | | | |
| | | | |
| | | | |
| | | | |
| | | | |
| | | | |
| | | | |
| | | | |
| | | | |
| | | | |
| | | | |
| | | | |
| | | | |
| | | | |
| | | | |

| EVENT: | | MAILING LIST | |
|---|---|---|---|
| LOCATION: | | DATE: TIME: | |

| NAME | EMAIL | PHONE | NOTE |
|---|---|---|---|
| | | | |
| | | | |
| | | | |
| | | | |
| | | | |
| | | | |
| | | | |
| | | | |
| | | | |
| | | | |
| | | | |
| | | | |
| | | | |
| | | | |
| | | | |
| | | | |
| | | | |
| | | | |
| | | | |
| | | | |
| | | | |
| | | | |
| | | | |
| | | | |
| | | | |
| | | | |
| | | | |

| EVENT: | | | MAILING LIST |
| :--- | :--- | :--- | :--- |
| LOCATION: | | | DATE:      TIME: |

| NAME | EMAIL | PHONE | NOTE |
| :--- | :--- | :--- | :--- |
| | | | |
| | | | |
| | | | |
| | | | |
| | | | |
| | | | |
| | | | |
| | | | |
| | | | |
| | | | |
| | | | |
| | | | |
| | | | |
| | | | |
| | | | |
| | | | |
| | | | |
| | | | |
| | | | |
| | | | |
| | | | |
| | | | |
| | | | |
| | | | |
| | | | |
| | | | |

| EVENT: | | | | MAILING LIST |
| --- | --- | --- | --- | --- |
| LOCATION: | | | DATE: | TIME: |

| NAME | EMAIL | PHONE | NOTE |
| --- | --- | --- | --- |
| | | | |
| | | | |
| | | | |
| | | | |
| | | | |
| | | | |
| | | | |
| | | | |
| | | | |
| | | | |
| | | | |
| | | | |
| | | | |
| | | | |
| | | | |
| | | | |
| | | | |
| | | | |
| | | | |
| | | | |
| | | | |
| | | | |
| | | | |

| EVENT: | | | MAILING LIST |
| LOCATION: | | | DATE:     TIME: |

| NAME | EMAIL | PHONE | NOTE |
|------|-------|-------|------|
|      |       |       |      |
|      |       |       |      |
|      |       |       |      |
|      |       |       |      |
|      |       |       |      |
|      |       |       |      |
|      |       |       |      |
|      |       |       |      |
|      |       |       |      |
|      |       |       |      |
|      |       |       |      |
|      |       |       |      |
|      |       |       |      |
|      |       |       |      |
|      |       |       |      |
|      |       |       |      |
|      |       |       |      |
|      |       |       |      |
|      |       |       |      |
|      |       |       |      |
|      |       |       |      |
|      |       |       |      |

**EVENT:**

**LOCATION:**

**MAILING LIST**

**DATE:**     **TIME:**

| NAME | EMAIL | PHONE | NOTE |
|------|-------|-------|------|
|      |       |       |      |
|      |       |       |      |
|      |       |       |      |
|      |       |       |      |
|      |       |       |      |
|      |       |       |      |
|      |       |       |      |
|      |       |       |      |
|      |       |       |      |
|      |       |       |      |
|      |       |       |      |
|      |       |       |      |
|      |       |       |      |
|      |       |       |      |
|      |       |       |      |
|      |       |       |      |
|      |       |       |      |
|      |       |       |      |
|      |       |       |      |
|      |       |       |      |
|      |       |       |      |
|      |       |       |      |
|      |       |       |      |

**EVENT:**

**LOCATION:**

**DATE:**     **TIME:**

| NAME | EMAIL | PHONE | NOTE |
|------|-------|-------|------|
|  |  |  |  |
|  |  |  |  |
|  |  |  |  |
|  |  |  |  |
|  |  |  |  |
|  |  |  |  |
|  |  |  |  |
|  |  |  |  |
|  |  |  |  |
|  |  |  |  |
|  |  |  |  |
|  |  |  |  |
|  |  |  |  |
|  |  |  |  |
|  |  |  |  |
|  |  |  |  |
|  |  |  |  |
|  |  |  |  |
|  |  |  |  |
|  |  |  |  |
|  |  |  |  |
|  |  |  |  |
|  |  |  |  |
|  |  |  |  |

| EVENT: | | | MAILING LIST |
|---|---|---|---|
| LOCATION: | | | DATE:    TIME: |

| NAME | EMAIL | PHONE | NOTE |
|---|---|---|---|
| | | | |
| | | | |
| | | | |
| | | | |
| | | | |
| | | | |
| | | | |
| | | | |
| | | | |
| | | | |
| | | | |
| | | | |
| | | | |
| | | | |
| | | | |
| | | | |
| | | | |
| | | | |
| | | | |
| | | | |
| | | | |
| | | | |

| EVENT: | | MAILING LIST | |
|---|---|---|---|
| LOCATION: | | DATE: | TIME: |

| NAME | EMAIL | PHONE | NOTE |
|---|---|---|---|
| | | | |
| | | | |
| | | | |
| | | | |
| | | | |
| | | | |
| | | | |
| | | | |
| | | | |
| | | | |
| | | | |
| | | | |
| | | | |
| | | | |
| | | | |
| | | | |
| | | | |
| | | | |
| | | | |
| | | | |
| | | | |
| | | | |
| | | | |

EVENT:

LOCATION:

DATE:     TIME:

| NAME | EMAIL | PHONE | NOTE |
|------|-------|-------|------|
|      |       |       |      |
|      |       |       |      |
|      |       |       |      |
|      |       |       |      |
|      |       |       |      |
|      |       |       |      |
|      |       |       |      |
|      |       |       |      |
|      |       |       |      |
|      |       |       |      |
|      |       |       |      |
|      |       |       |      |
|      |       |       |      |
|      |       |       |      |
|      |       |       |      |
|      |       |       |      |
|      |       |       |      |
|      |       |       |      |
|      |       |       |      |
|      |       |       |      |
|      |       |       |      |
|      |       |       |      |
|      |       |       |      |

| EVENT: | | | | MAILING LIST |
|--------|--|--|--|--------------|

| LOCATION: | | DATE: | TIME: |
|-----------|--|-------|-------|

| NAME | EMAIL | PHONE | NOTE |
|------|-------|-------|------|
|  |  |  |  |
|  |  |  |  |
|  |  |  |  |
|  |  |  |  |
|  |  |  |  |
|  |  |  |  |
|  |  |  |  |
|  |  |  |  |
|  |  |  |  |
|  |  |  |  |
|  |  |  |  |
|  |  |  |  |
|  |  |  |  |
|  |  |  |  |
|  |  |  |  |
|  |  |  |  |
|  |  |  |  |
|  |  |  |  |
|  |  |  |  |
|  |  |  |  |
|  |  |  |  |
|  |  |  |  |
|  |  |  |  |
|  |  |  |  |

| EVENT: | | | MAILING LIST |
| --- | --- | --- | --- |
| LOCATION: | | | DATE:     TIME: |

| NAME | EMAIL | PHONE | NOTE |
| --- | --- | --- | --- |
| | | | |
| | | | |
| | | | |
| | | | |
| | | | |
| | | | |
| | | | |
| | | | |
| | | | |
| | | | |
| | | | |
| | | | |
| | | | |
| | | | |
| | | | |
| | | | |
| | | | |
| | | | |
| | | | |
| | | | |
| | | | |
| | | | |
| | | | |

| EVENT: | | | MAILING LIST |
| --- | --- | --- | --- |
| LOCATION: | | | DATE:    TIME: |

| NAME | EMAIL | PHONE | NOTE |
| --- | --- | --- | --- |
|  |  |  |  |
|  |  |  |  |
|  |  |  |  |
|  |  |  |  |
|  |  |  |  |
|  |  |  |  |
|  |  |  |  |
|  |  |  |  |
|  |  |  |  |
|  |  |  |  |
|  |  |  |  |
|  |  |  |  |
|  |  |  |  |
|  |  |  |  |
|  |  |  |  |
|  |  |  |  |
|  |  |  |  |
|  |  |  |  |
|  |  |  |  |
|  |  |  |  |
|  |  |  |  |
|  |  |  |  |
|  |  |  |  |
|  |  |  |  |

**EVENT:**

**LOCATION:**

## MAILING LIST

**DATE:**     **TIME:**

| NAME | EMAIL | PHONE | NOTE |
|------|-------|-------|------|
|      |       |       |      |
|      |       |       |      |
|      |       |       |      |
|      |       |       |      |
|      |       |       |      |
|      |       |       |      |
|      |       |       |      |
|      |       |       |      |
|      |       |       |      |
|      |       |       |      |
|      |       |       |      |
|      |       |       |      |
|      |       |       |      |
|      |       |       |      |
|      |       |       |      |
|      |       |       |      |
|      |       |       |      |
|      |       |       |      |
|      |       |       |      |
|      |       |       |      |
|      |       |       |      |
|      |       |       |      |
|      |       |       |      |
|      |       |       |      |

| EVENT: | | | |
|---|---|---|---|

| LOCATION: | | | |
|---|---|---|---|

DATE:     TIME:

| NAME | EMAIL | PHONE | NOTE |
|---|---|---|---|
| | | | |
| | | | |
| | | | |
| | | | |
| | | | |
| | | | |
| | | | |
| | | | |
| | | | |
| | | | |
| | | | |
| | | | |
| | | | |
| | | | |
| | | | |
| | | | |
| | | | |
| | | | |
| | | | |
| | | | |
| | | | |
| | | | |
| | | | |
| | | | |
| | | | |

**EVENT:**

**LOCATION:**

## MAILING LIST

**DATE:**     **TIME:**

| NAME | EMAIL | PHONE | NOTE |
|------|-------|-------|------|
|      |       |       |      |
|      |       |       |      |
|      |       |       |      |
|      |       |       |      |
|      |       |       |      |
|      |       |       |      |
|      |       |       |      |
|      |       |       |      |
|      |       |       |      |
|      |       |       |      |
|      |       |       |      |
|      |       |       |      |
|      |       |       |      |
|      |       |       |      |
|      |       |       |      |
|      |       |       |      |
|      |       |       |      |
|      |       |       |      |
|      |       |       |      |
|      |       |       |      |
|      |       |       |      |
|      |       |       |      |
|      |       |       |      |

**EVENT:**

**LOCATION:**

## MAILING LIST

**DATE:**     **TIME:**

| NAME | EMAIL | PHONE | NOTE |
|------|-------|-------|------|
|  |  |  |  |
|  |  |  |  |
|  |  |  |  |
|  |  |  |  |
|  |  |  |  |
|  |  |  |  |
|  |  |  |  |
|  |  |  |  |
|  |  |  |  |
|  |  |  |  |
|  |  |  |  |
|  |  |  |  |
|  |  |  |  |
|  |  |  |  |
|  |  |  |  |
|  |  |  |  |
|  |  |  |  |
|  |  |  |  |
|  |  |  |  |
|  |  |  |  |
|  |  |  |  |
|  |  |  |  |
|  |  |  |  |
|  |  |  |  |

**EVENT:**

**LOCATION:**

**MAILING LIST**

**DATE:**     **TIME:**

| NAME | EMAIL | PHONE | NOTE |
|------|-------|-------|------|
|      |       |       |      |
|      |       |       |      |
|      |       |       |      |
|      |       |       |      |
|      |       |       |      |
|      |       |       |      |
|      |       |       |      |
|      |       |       |      |
|      |       |       |      |
|      |       |       |      |
|      |       |       |      |
|      |       |       |      |
|      |       |       |      |
|      |       |       |      |
|      |       |       |      |
|      |       |       |      |
|      |       |       |      |
|      |       |       |      |
|      |       |       |      |
|      |       |       |      |
|      |       |       |      |
|      |       |       |      |

**EVENT:**

**LOCATION:**

**DATE:**    **TIME:**

| NAME | EMAIL | PHONE | NOTE |
|------|-------|-------|------|
|  |  |  |  |
|  |  |  |  |
|  |  |  |  |
|  |  |  |  |
|  |  |  |  |
|  |  |  |  |
|  |  |  |  |
|  |  |  |  |
|  |  |  |  |
|  |  |  |  |
|  |  |  |  |
|  |  |  |  |
|  |  |  |  |
|  |  |  |  |
|  |  |  |  |
|  |  |  |  |
|  |  |  |  |
|  |  |  |  |
|  |  |  |  |
|  |  |  |  |
|  |  |  |  |

| EVENT: | | | MAILING LIST |
|---|---|---|---|

| LOCATION: | | DATE: | TIME: |
|---|---|---|---|

| NAME | EMAIL | PHONE | NOTE |
|---|---|---|---|
| | | | |
| | | | |
| | | | |
| | | | |
| | | | |
| | | | |
| | | | |
| | | | |
| | | | |
| | | | |
| | | | |
| | | | |
| | | | |
| | | | |
| | | | |
| | | | |
| | | | |
| | | | |
| | | | |
| | | | |
| | | | |
| | | | |
| | | | |
| | | | |
| | | | |
| | | | |
| | | | |

EVENT:

LOCATION:

**MAILING LIST**

DATE:    TIME:

| NAME | EMAIL | PHONE | NOTE |
|------|-------|-------|------|
|      |       |       |      |
|      |       |       |      |
|      |       |       |      |
|      |       |       |      |
|      |       |       |      |
|      |       |       |      |
|      |       |       |      |
|      |       |       |      |
|      |       |       |      |
|      |       |       |      |
|      |       |       |      |
|      |       |       |      |
|      |       |       |      |
|      |       |       |      |
|      |       |       |      |
|      |       |       |      |
|      |       |       |      |
|      |       |       |      |
|      |       |       |      |
|      |       |       |      |
|      |       |       |      |
|      |       |       |      |

**EVENT:**

**LOCATION:**

**MAILING LIST**

**DATE:**    **TIME:**

| NAME | EMAIL | PHONE | NOTE |
|------|-------|-------|------|
|      |       |       |      |
|      |       |       |      |
|      |       |       |      |
|      |       |       |      |
|      |       |       |      |
|      |       |       |      |
|      |       |       |      |
|      |       |       |      |
|      |       |       |      |
|      |       |       |      |
|      |       |       |      |
|      |       |       |      |
|      |       |       |      |
|      |       |       |      |
|      |       |       |      |
|      |       |       |      |
|      |       |       |      |
|      |       |       |      |
|      |       |       |      |
|      |       |       |      |
|      |       |       |      |
|      |       |       |      |

| EVENT: | | | MAILING LIST |
| --- | --- | --- | --- |
| LOCATION: | | | DATE: TIME: |

| NAME | EMAIL | PHONE | NOTE |
| --- | --- | --- | --- |
| | | | |
| | | | |
| | | | |
| | | | |
| | | | |
| | | | |
| | | | |
| | | | |
| | | | |
| | | | |
| | | | |
| | | | |
| | | | |
| | | | |
| | | | |
| | | | |
| | | | |
| | | | |
| | | | |
| | | | |
| | | | |
| | | | |
| | | | |
| | | | |

| EVENT: | | | MAILING LIST |
|---|---|---|---|
| LOCATION: | | | DATE: TIME: |

| NAME | EMAIL | PHONE | NOTE |
|---|---|---|---|
| | | | |
| | | | |
| | | | |
| | | | |
| | | | |
| | | | |
| | | | |
| | | | |
| | | | |
| | | | |
| | | | |
| | | | |
| | | | |
| | | | |
| | | | |
| | | | |
| | | | |
| | | | |
| | | | |
| | | | |
| | | | |
| | | | |
| | | | |

EVENT:

LOCATION:

## MAILING LIST

DATE:      TIME:

| NAME | EMAIL | PHONE | NOTE |
|------|-------|-------|------|
|      |       |       |      |
|      |       |       |      |
|      |       |       |      |
|      |       |       |      |
|      |       |       |      |
|      |       |       |      |
|      |       |       |      |
|      |       |       |      |
|      |       |       |      |
|      |       |       |      |
|      |       |       |      |
|      |       |       |      |
|      |       |       |      |
|      |       |       |      |
|      |       |       |      |
|      |       |       |      |
|      |       |       |      |
|      |       |       |      |
|      |       |       |      |
|      |       |       |      |
|      |       |       |      |
|      |       |       |      |
|      |       |       |      |

**EVENT:**

**LOCATION:**

## MAILING LIST

**DATE:**     **TIME:**

| NAME | EMAIL | PHONE | NOTE |
|------|-------|-------|------|
|      |       |       |      |
|      |       |       |      |
|      |       |       |      |
|      |       |       |      |
|      |       |       |      |
|      |       |       |      |
|      |       |       |      |
|      |       |       |      |
|      |       |       |      |
|      |       |       |      |
|      |       |       |      |
|      |       |       |      |
|      |       |       |      |
|      |       |       |      |
|      |       |       |      |
|      |       |       |      |
|      |       |       |      |
|      |       |       |      |
|      |       |       |      |
|      |       |       |      |
|      |       |       |      |
|      |       |       |      |
|      |       |       |      |
|      |       |       |      |

| EVENT: | | | MAILING LIST |
|---|---|---|---|
| LOCATION: | | | DATE: TIME: |

| NAME | EMAIL | PHONE | NOTE |
|---|---|---|---|
| | | | |
| | | | |
| | | | |
| | | | |
| | | | |
| | | | |
| | | | |
| | | | |
| | | | |
| | | | |
| | | | |
| | | | |
| | | | |
| | | | |
| | | | |
| | | | |
| | | | |
| | | | |
| | | | |
| | | | |
| | | | |
| | | | |
| | | | |
| | | | |

| | | | | |
|---|---|---|---|---|
| **SUNDAY** | ◯ | ◯ | ◯ | ◯ |
| **MONDAY** | ◯ | ◯ | ◯ | ◯ |
| **TUESDAY** | ◯ | ◯ | ◯ | ◯ |
| **WEDNESDAY** | ◯ | ◯ | ◯ | ◯ |
| **THURSDAY** | ◯ | ◯ | ◯ | ◯ |
| **FRIDAY** | ◯ | ◯ | ◯ | ◯ |
| **SATURDAY** | ◯ | ◯ | ◯ | ◯ |

**YEAR :** [ ] **MONTH:** [ ]

| | | | | |
|---|---|---|---|---|
| **SUNDAY** | ◯ | ◯ | ◯ | ◯ |
| **MONDAY** | ◯ | ◯ | ◯ | ◯ |
| **TUESDAY** | ◯ | ◯ | ◯ | ◯ |
| **WEDNESDAY** | ◯ | ◯ | ◯ | ◯ |
| **THURSDAY** | ◯ | ◯ | ◯ | ◯ |
| **FRIDAY** | ◯ | ◯ | ◯ | ◯ |
| **SATURDAY** | ◯ | ◯ | ◯ | ◯ |

**YEAR :** [ ]   **MONTH:** [ ]

| | | | | |
|---|---|---|---|---|
| **SUNDAY** | ◯ | ◯ | ◯ | ◯ |
| **MONDAY** | ◯ | ◯ | ◯ | ◯ |
| **TUESDAY** | ◯ | ◯ | ◯ | ◯ |
| **WEDNESDAY** | ◯ | ◯ | ◯ | ◯ |
| **THURSDAY** | ◯ | ◯ | ◯ | ◯ |
| **FRIDAY** | ◯ | ◯ | ◯ | ◯ |
| **SATURDAY** | ◯ | ◯ | ◯ | ◯ |

**YEAR :**  **MONTH:**

| | | | | |
|---|---|---|---|---|
| **SUNDAY** | ◯ | ◯ | ◯ | ◯ |
| **MONDAY** | ◯ | ◯ | ◯ | ◯ |
| **TUESDAY** | ◯ | ◯ | ◯ | ◯ |
| **WEDNESDAY** | ◯ | ◯ | ◯ | ◯ |
| **THURSDAY** | ◯ | ◯ | ◯ | ◯ |
| **FRIDAY** | ◯ | ◯ | ◯ | ◯ |
| **SATURDAY** | ◯ | ◯ | ◯ | ◯ |

**YEAR :** [          ]     **MONTH:** [          ]

| | | | | |
|---|---|---|---|---|
| SUNDAY | ◯ | ◯ | ◯ | ◯ |
| MONDAY | ◯ | ◯ | ◯ | ◯ |
| TUESDAY | ◯ | ◯ | ◯ | ◯ |
| WEDNESDAY | ◯ | ◯ | ◯ | ◯ |
| THURSDAY | ◯ | ◯ | ◯ | ◯ |
| FRIDAY | ◯ | ◯ | ◯ | ◯ |
| SATURDAY | ◯ | ◯ | ◯ | ◯ |

YEAR : 　　　　　　　MONTH: 　　　　　

| | | | | |
|---|---|---|---|---|
| **SUNDAY** | ◯ | ◯ | ◯ | ◯ |
| **MONDAY** | ◯ | ◯ | ◯ | ◯ |
| **TUESDAY** | ◯ | ◯ | ◯ | ◯ |
| **WEDNESDAY** | ◯ | ◯ | ◯ | ◯ |
| **THURSDAY** | ◯ | ◯ | ◯ | ◯ |
| **FRIDAY** | ◯ | ◯ | ◯ | ◯ |
| **SATURDAY** | ◯ | ◯ | ◯ | ◯ |

**YEAR :**

**MONTH:**

| | | | | |
|---|---|---|---|---|
| **SUNDAY** | ○ | ○ | ○ | ○ |
| **MONDAY** | ○ | ○ | ○ | ○ |
| **TUESDAY** | ○ | ○ | ○ | ○ |
| **WEDNESDAY** | ○ | ○ | ○ | ○ |
| **THURSDAY** | ○ | ○ | ○ | ○ |
| **FRIDAY** | ○ | ○ | ○ | ○ |
| **SATURDAY** | ○ | ○ | ○ | ○ |

| | | | | |
|---|---|---|---|---|
| **SUNDAY** | ◯ | ◯ | ◯ | ◯ |
| **MONDAY** | ◯ | ◯ | ◯ | ◯ |
| **TUESDAY** | ◯ | ◯ | ◯ | ◯ |
| **WEDNESDAY** | ◯ | ◯ | ◯ | ◯ |
| **THURSDAY** | ◯ | ◯ | ◯ | ◯ |
| **FRIDAY** | ◯ | ◯ | ◯ | ◯ |
| **SATURDAY** | ◯ | ◯ | ◯ | ◯ |

**YEAR :** [          ]     **MONTH:** [          ]

| SUNDAY | | | |
|---|---|---|---|
| ○ | ○ | ○ | ○ |

| MONDAY | | | |
|---|---|---|---|
| ○ | ○ | ○ | ○ |

| TUESDAY | | | |
|---|---|---|---|
| ○ | ○ | ○ | ○ |

| WEDNESDAY | | | |
|---|---|---|---|
| ○ | ○ | ○ | ○ |

| THURSDAY | | | |
|---|---|---|---|
| ○ | ○ | ○ | ○ |

| FRIDAY | | | |
|---|---|---|---|
| ○ | ○ | ○ | ○ |

| SATURDAY | | | |
|---|---|---|---|
| ○ | ○ | ○ | ○ |

| YEAR : | | MONTH: | |
|---|---|---|---|

| | | | | |
|---|---|---|---|---|
| **SUNDAY** | ◯ | ◯ | ◯ | ◯ |
| **MONDAY** | ◯ | ◯ | ◯ | ◯ |
| **TUESDAY** | ◯ | ◯ | ◯ | ◯ |
| **WEDNESDAY** | ◯ | ◯ | ◯ | ◯ |
| **THURSDAY** | ◯ | ◯ | ◯ | ◯ |
| **FRIDAY** | ◯ | ◯ | ◯ | ◯ |
| **SATURDAY** | ◯ | ◯ | ◯ | ◯ |

**YEAR :** [ ] **MONTH:** [ ]

| | | | |
|---|---|---|---|
| **SUNDAY** ( ) | ( ) | ( ) | ( ) |
| **MONDAY** ( ) | ( ) | ( ) | ( ) |
| **TUESDAY** ( ) | ( ) | ( ) | ( ) |
| **WEDNESDAY** ( ) | ( ) | ( ) | ( ) |
| **THURSDAY** ( ) | ( ) | ( ) | ( ) |
| **FRIDAY** ( ) | ( ) | ( ) | ( ) |
| **SATURDAY** ( ) | ( ) | ( ) | ( ) |

**YEAR :** [ ] **MONTH:** [ ]

| | | | |
|---|---|---|---|
| **SUNDAY** ○ | ○ | ○ | ○ |
| **MONDAY** ○ | ○ | ○ | ○ |
| **TUESDAY** ○ | ○ | ○ | ○ |
| **WEDNESDAY** ○ | ○ | ○ | ○ |
| **THURSDAY** ○ | ○ | ○ | ○ |
| **FRIDAY** ○ | ○ | ○ | ○ |
| **SATURDAY** ○ | ○ | ○ | ○ |

Made in the USA
Coppell, TX
13 September 2023